Fairy Fay's Bad Day

Level 4B

Written by Deborah Chancellor
Illustrated by Kimberley Scott

What is synthetic phonics?

Synthetic phonics teaches children to recognise the sounds of letters and to blend (synthesise) them together to make whole words.

Understanding sound/letter relationships gives children the confidence and ability to read unfamiliar words, without having to rely on memory or guesswork; this helps them to progress towards independent reading.

Did you know? Spoken English uses more than 40 speech sounds. Each sound is called a *phoneme*. Some phonemes relate to a single letter (d-o-g) and others to combinations of letters (sh-ar-p). When a phoneme is written down it is called a *grapheme*. Teaching these sounds, matching them to their written form and sounding out words for reading is the basis of synthetic phonics.

Consultant

I love reading phonics has been created in consultation with language expert Abigail Steel. She has a background in teaching and teacher training and is a respected expert in the field of synthetic phonics. Abigail Steel is a regular contributor to educational publications. Her international education consultancy supports parents and teachers in the promotion of literacy skills.

Reading tips

This book focuses on the ai sound, made with the letters ay and ey, as in play and they.

Tricky words in this book

Any words in bold may have unusual spellings or are new and have not yet been introduced.

> **Tricky words in this book:**
>
> ## fairies behave alone wants change more

Extra ways to have fun with this book

After the reader has read the story, ask them questions about what they have just read:

What does Fay turn the Queen into?
What makes Fay stop being a bad fairy?

Us rabbits love to frolic and play, can you spot us in the book?

A pronunciation guide

This grid contains the sounds used in the stories in levels 4, 5 and 6 and a guide on how to say them. /a/ represents the sounds made, rather than the letters in a word.

/ai/ as in game	/ai/ as in play/they	/ee/ as in leaf/these	/ee/ as in he
/igh/ as in kite/light	/igh/ as in find/sky	/oa/ as in home	/oa/ as in snow
/oa/ as in cold	/y+oo/ as in cube/music/new	long /oo/ as in flute/crew/blue	/oi/ as in boy
/er/ as in bird/hurt	/or/ as in snore/oar/door	/or/ as in dawn/sauce/walk	/e/ as in head
/e/ as in said/any	/ou/ as in cow	/u/ as in touch	/air/ as in hare/bear/there
/eer/ as in deer/here/cashier	/t/ as in tripped/skipped	/d/ as in rained	/j/ as in gent/gin/gym
/j/ as in barge/hedge	/s/ as in cent/circus/cyst	/s/ as in prince	/s/ as in house
/ch/ as in itch/catch	/w/ as in white	/h/ as in who	/r/ as in write/rhino

Sounds in this story are
highlighted in the grid.

/f/ as in phone	/f/ as in rough	/ul/ as in pencil/hospital	/z/ as in fries/cheese/breeze
/n/ as in knot/gnome/engine	/m/ as in welcome /thumb/column	/g/ as in guitar/ghost	/zh/ as in vision/beige
/k/ as in chord	/k/ as in plaque/bouquet	/nk/ as in uncle	/ks/ as in box/books/ducks/cakes
/a/ and /o/ as in hat/what	/e/ and /ee/ as in bed/he	/i/ and /igh/ as in fin/find	/o/ and /oa/ as in hot/cold
/u/ and short /oo/ as in but/put	/ee/, /e/ and /ai/ as in eat/bread/break	/igh/, /ee/ and /e/ as in tie/field/friend	/ou/ and /oa/ as in cow/blow
/ou/, /oa/ and /oo/ as in out/shoulder/could	/i/ and /ai/ as in money/they	/c/ and /s/ as in cat/cent	/y/, /igh/ and /i/ as in yes/sky/myth
/g/ and /j/ as in got/giant	/ch/, /c/ and /sh/ as in chin/school/chef	/er/, /air/ and /eer/ as in earth/bear/ears	/u/, /ou/ and /oa/ as in plough/dough

Be careful not to add an 'uh' sound to 's', 't', 'p',
'c', 'h', 'r', 'm', 'd', 'g', 'l', 'f' and 'b'. For example,
say 'fff' not 'fuh' and 'sss' not 'suh'.

Fay is a bad fairy.
All day long, she makes
wicked spells.

She preys on good **fairies**.

8

The Fairy Queen is cross
with Fay.

"Hey! This is no way to **behave**!"
she cries. "Just play, Fay!"

But Fay disobeys the
Fairy Queen.
"Buzz off, okay!" Fay says.

Zap! Fay turns the Queen into a frog.

"Yay!" says Fay. "You can stay
that way today!"

The Fairy Queen hops away.

The fairies are not happy.
They stomp off with the Queen,
and stay away from Fay.

Fay is **alone**.
She has no playmates now.

"Hey, perhaps being bad is not the way!" she thinks.

Fay is sorry. She **wants** to **change** her ways.

Zap! Fay makes a good spell
at last...

The frog is a Queen again.
Fay chucks her wand away.

"No **more** bad spells!" she says.
"Let's just play!"

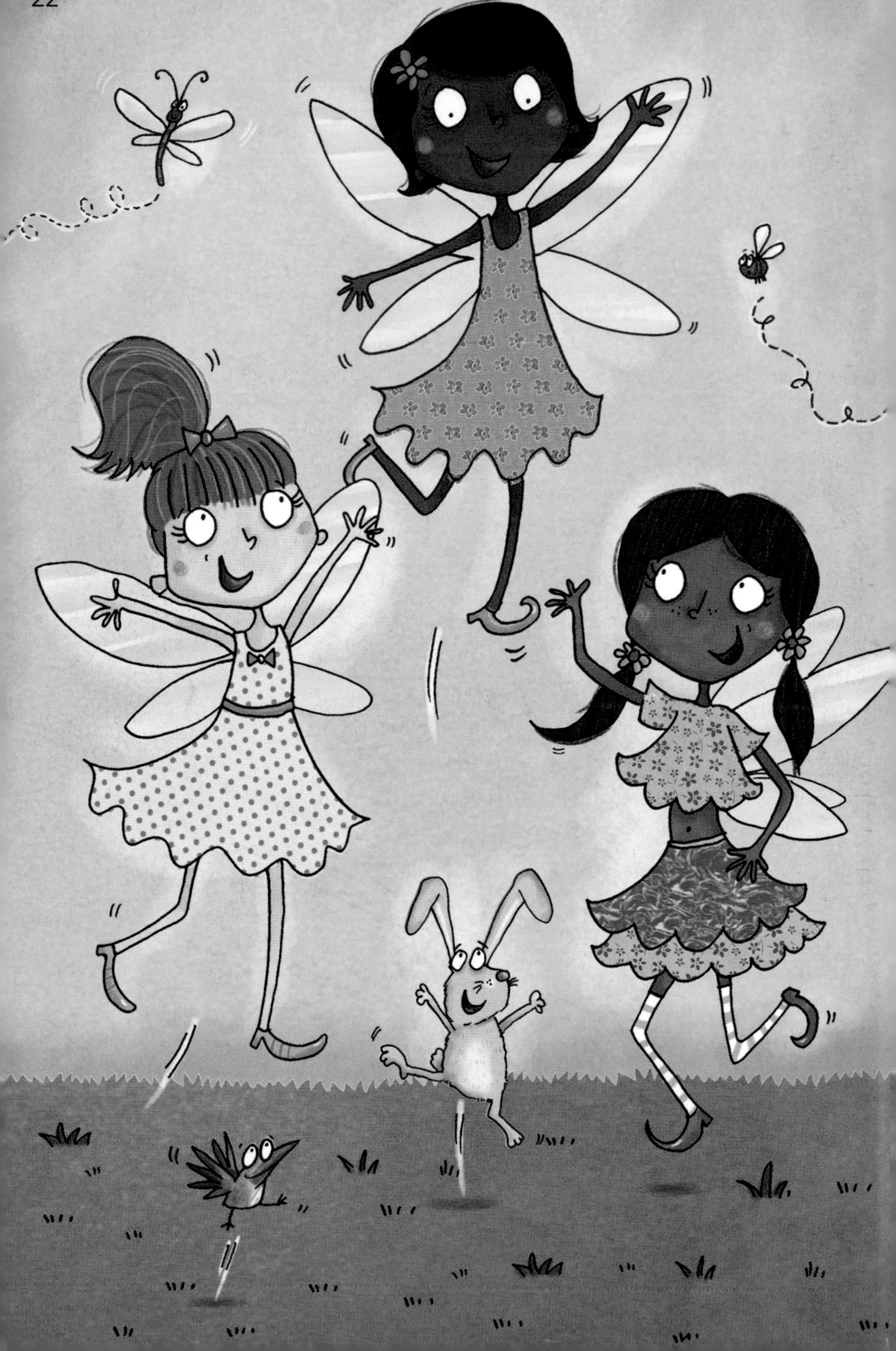

The fairies cheer.
"Hooray!" they say.
They do not stay mad at Fay.

OVER **48** TITLES IN SIX LEVELS
Abigail Steel recommends...

Other titles to enjoy from Level 4

The Maze — I love reading phonics — 978-1-84898-559-9

Fairy Fay's Bad Day — I love reading phonics — 978-1-84898-560-5

Pirate School — I love reading phonics — 978-1-84898-566-7

Some titles from Level 5

Snapped by Sam — I love reading phonics — 978-1-84898-561-2

Max's Trip — I love reading phonics — 978-1-84898-562-9

George the Genius Gerbil — I love reading phonics — 978-1-84898-567-4

Some titles from Level 6

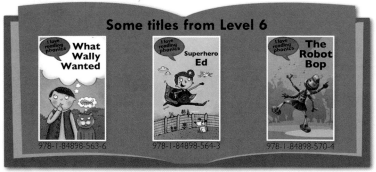

What Wally Wanted — I love reading phonics — 978-1-84898-563-6

Superhero Ed — I love reading phonics — 978-1-84898-564-3

The Robot Bop — I love reading phonics — 978-1-84898-570-4

An Hachette UK Company
www.hachette.co.uk

Copyright © Octopus Publishing Group Ltd 2012
First published in Great Britain in 2012 by TickTock, an imprint of Octopus Publishing Group Ltd,
Endeavour House, 189 Shaftesbury Avenue, London WC2H 8JY.
www.octopusbooks.co.uk

ISBN 978 1 84898 560 5

Printed and bound in China
10 9 8 7 6 5 4 3 2 1